I wish I would have had this book when I was a freshman! Laura offers a great balance of no-brainer decisions and surprisingly practical gems, especially for the young student unaccustomed to living on a budget and living creatively.

—Sarah J. Peterson, 2010 Graduate

We'll never know how many college degrees were achieved, credit ratings kept stable, or anxieties prevented by this little book. But I hope the happy ending is yours. Do read the book. Laura Gilbert knows whereof she speaks.

—Beverly Pierce, MLS, MA, RN, parent

Laura Gilbert's book is a "must read" for both students and parents before submitting your college applications. Loaded with solid, practical advice on planning for the cost of higher education while reducing expenses and avoiding high student debt, this book can save you thousands of dollars before you set foot on campus.

—Denise Stephens, Customized Training & Continuing Education, Minnesota State Colleges & Universities

Dr. Gilbert offers practical, valuable, and humorous advice for students and parents. This book belongs on the "must read" list of every current student, potential student, and their parents.

—Julie Tschida, Professor

How to Save $50,000 on College

Laura H. Gilbert, Ph.D.

 Published through Createspace.com, June 2011.

Contact the author at laura@saveonyoureducation.com.

To purchase copies of this book and for information about the author, visit https://www.createspace.com/3574189.

Cover and interior design: Christy J. P. Barker

For my Dad

Who taught me the true value of a dime
and that life works best on a budget.

Acknowledgments

Special thanks to Beverly Pierce for her careful eye and librarian's logic, and to Beth Dinndorf for sharing her years of expertise as a student loan executive. This book is a much stronger "read" because of their contributions. Thank you both.

Thanks also to my book designer, Christy J. P. Barker. The whimsical cover and appealing layout demonstrate Christy's ability to visually match the author's voice.

Thanks to my children, Angela, Alex, Karina and Tony, for letting me walk this path with you. Little can match the joy of watching your child discover and embrace his or her dreams.

Finally, a special thank you goes to students and parents who shared with me their stories and concerns about paying for college. This book was written for you. May the college experience be everything you want; and may you graduate with money to spare.

Table of Contents

Introduction

What is college worth?

As hard as we try, it is impossible to place an accurate value on the personal, intellectual and long-term career benefits of a college education.

Decades of data indicate that adult life is largely defined by one's level of education, what you study, where you go and who you meet during college. And there is widespread agreement that college is the clearest path to a decent paying job. Sadly, many graduates also face crushing debt loads that can negatively impact wallet and psyche for years to come. That doesn't have to be you.

I believe every student has the opportunity to make choices that keep college costs in line with their financial objectives and the practical value of their diploma.

College should define your adult life by what you learn, not by what you owe.

Every student's situation is unique—to a point. A great cost-saving tactic for Tristan might be horrible for Finn. When I work with a student or family, we identify tactics that work for them. Some ideas in these chapters will be great for you. Other ideas, not so much. Use what works and cross out the rest.

My objective is to help you get the educational experience you want while avoiding an unreasonable debt load, especially the kind that can cost blood down the road. Here is the story that pushed me to write this book. Don't let this be you.

> Cassie and Mark met in college and married after graduation. When I met them they had just turned 30. Cassie was working part-time from home to save on daycare expenses. Mark's job at a non-profit matched their values but not their bills. Their biggest stressor: more than $80,000 in undergraduate student loans. An early default on federal loans disqualified either of them from federal funds to retrain for a better job. Having exhausted other options, Mark made their minimum loan payments by selling his plasma at a local blood bank while he sought a better job.

College is expensive. It always has been. A college education is likely to be the second most expensive purchase in your lifetime, the first being a house, although current trends may temporarily reverse those two.

The estimated cost to earn a bachelor's degree at a large state school can top $100,000; $200,000 or more at many private schools. Even families with college savings and good jobs struggle to imagine how to make it happen.

In addition, higher education is no longer a one-time event. The cost of college used to be measured against the benefit of a lifetime career. Not anymore. While the first degree provides a foundation for an initial career, expect to return for training or a new career at least once down the road. Don't overspend on the first round.

But, is a degree really necessary?

According to economist and financial guru Chris Farrell, a post-secondary education is "more valuable than ever."[1]

---

1. Farrell, Chris, *A College Degree is Still Worth It*, http://blogs.cfed.org/cfed_news_clips/, Accessed March 20, 2011.

But what about Bill Gates and Mark Zuckerberg? First, they didn't actually skip school. Plus, don't count on their good fortune. If your parents or grandparents did well with no more than a high school degree and think you can do the same, point out that in 1950, 80% of jobs were categorized as unskilled, requiring no more than a high school diploma, if that. In 2010, 85% were skilled; quite the reversal. National reports suggest more than 60% of jobs now require college education—a number that continues to grow.

Does that mean students must choose between 10–25 years of crushing student loan debt or a life of minimum wage jobs? No! There are many ways to get a great education without spending (or borrowing) enough to buy lunch for France.

Throughout this book you'll learn simple and timeless tips to get the product you seek (a degree or other credential) for a reasonable price. Most depend only on you, neither on good luck (scholarships) nor Congress (special federal programs), although I've included a few thoughts on those, too.

Sounds like something a smart person like you would do, right? You wouldn't pay $100 for shoes you could get for $40 unless they really were different, right? Think about it. Why not? Does your answer have anything to do with the value to you? The same goes for education.

For the record, I have used, witnessed or heard convincing testimony about every tip in this book. These little ideas have saved thousands of dollars in upfront cash and student loan payments for everyone in my family as well as for countless friends and clients.

What about scholarships, loans and credit cards?

You'll learn how to think out-of-the-box when it comes to scholarships. And, you'll learn how to choose good loans, look out for poor loans and how to decide a reasonable debt load and monthly loan payment that works for you.

There are many other excellent books and websites that can help you find and apply for specific scholarships and student loans. I teach you what questions to ask and how to decide what is right for you. For more details, financial aid officers, guidance counselors, banking professionals and educational tax experts are your best bet.

My entire philosophy on credit cards can be summed up in eleven words:

Have only one card. Pay off the balance each month. Period.

Chapter One presents the basics. What do college costs include? Why do college costs vary so much from one student to the next? How can you be the one with less debt? What is the college selling? How does their brand affect you? How do you affect their brand?

Chapters Two and Three tackle how to save on the big things (tuition) and the little things (fun) without sacrificing the educational or social experience you want from college.

Chapter Four takes a look at the largest and longest-lasting college expense: student loans.

Chapter Five was written for those who like to skip to the big messages.

Chapter Six is a bonus for students who are already considering graduate school.

The final section shows you how to create a customized, high-level, reasonable College Budget and apply it to a sample financial aid award letter. Blank forms are included for your use. Finally, I show you how to use the model that sent four kids and me to college.

How much will you save with these tips? How much do you save by being a safe driver? You'll never know for sure. Part depends on chance. Part depends on the vehicle you choose. And a big part depends on learning safe driving tips before you get behind the wheel.

The same goes for financing a college degree. By understanding a few ins and outs before you start, including some safe financing tips about loans, you can get the most from your college experience for a cost that is reasonable for you.

And finally, before we dig in, remember this:

How much a college charges for a degree is the college's decision.

How much a family commits to pay for college is the family's decision.

Don't confuse the two.

Have fun. Don't skimp where it matters. Save money where it doesn't. Learn, learn, learn.

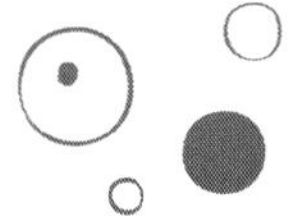

Chapter One: Managing College Costs

Cost Defined

What does college cost? Good question.

A major challenge for students and families is the fact that there is no single, definitive answer to this question. Even students at the same college incur different costs. Consider this:

> If Max and Ariel go to Jamba Juice and order the same drink, the costs are identical.
>
> If Max and Ariel go to the same college the same year, with the same financial aid package and graduate with the same major, their individual cost for college will be different.
>
> Why? Jamba Juice products and prices are fixed. Most college costs are not.

College marketing materials list their cost for tuition, fees, room and board. If they don't, run. Institutional costs should be easy to find. This is the full-pay, cash price for the listed items in a given year. It is a valuable starting point for comparing program price tags. However, it fails to consider scholarship awards, tuition increases, four years of personal expenditures and long-term interest on student loans. This figure also fails to acknowledge the flexibility of many college expenses.

A better place to start is to put the marketing materials to the side and instead define the <u>cost of college to you</u> (the target for this book) versus the <u>total cost of college</u> (the number you hear in the news and then some).

The cost of college to you includes every penny spent or borrowed to earn your degree. This includes cash or loans contributed by you, your parents, grandparents, siblings and any generous donor who slips a $20 in your graduation card.

As a prospective student you should also understand the total cost of college. This number represents the actual cost of your degree. It includes the total cost to you *plus* all funding you receive but don't have to repay, such as scholarships and grants.

Plus, tuition rarely covers 100% of a college's cost to educate you. Alumni contributions, government funds and the occasional business partnership provide the rest. Remember this when it is your turn to make an alumni donation.

How do you define college costs?

College Models and Formats

Every college falls into one of three models:

Public—Regulated by a state and funded in part by state dollars, the school name may include state (University of Delaware), although not necessarily so. (Slippery Rock University is public whereas Colorado College is private.)

Private—Generally not-for-profit entities, may be affiliated with a religion (often transparently so), funded by tuition, alumni donations, gifts and other sources. Harvard, Boston University, Hobart & William Smith, and Dordt College are private colleges.

For-profit—Set up as a for-profit business, the largest for-profit schools are publicly traded. If a for-profit is best for you, confirm with a public or private college that the for-profit's accreditation will allow credits to transfer. Keep your options open.

Every course falls into one of three formats:

Face-to-face—This is the traditional classroom course. You and the professor are both physically present.

Online—You and the professor are both online. This is a convenient option (although not necessarily less expensive) for many non-traditional students.

Blended—Many courses now include face-to-face and online elements in varying proportions.

Cost is not entirely based on model or format. Princeton, MIT and Harvard are three of the most expensive colleges and three of the most generous with scholarships. Don't limit your options. Apply to programs of interest, see what they offer and do the math. The most expensive college for Victor might be the cheapest for Tea.

The same goes for format. The cost for an online class through a private college might be a better deal for you than a face-to-face summer class at a community college if, for example, the online course allows you to take a job or to graduate early. You decide.

Every college is right for someone.
Choose the one that is right for you.

Managing Costs—Part I: The Basics

There are two basic ways to save money:

(a) Collect it

(b) DON'T SPEND IT

Collecting money is the easier method. Just like collecting baseball cards, collecting money involves acquiring it by some means (gifts, work, barter) and depositing it somewhere (bank, drawer, mattress.) No matter where it is, you can easily measure how much you saved.

Saving money on the cost of college involves *spending less* money than you might otherwise. This is hard because you can't easily see your achievement, unless you calculate the money not spent and put it in a jar . . . unlikely. How do you know when to celebrate? What motivates you to not spend?

Motivation to save money on college comes from understanding the long-term benefits of low loan debt. Fear of high loan payments also works. More in Chapter Four—*Student Loans.*

How do you spend less when many college costs are non-optional? By creating a college budget and increasing your awareness of expenses and options so you can make healthy choices.

College costs fall into three categories:

- *Obvious costs:* tuition, housing, food
- *Sneaky costs:* everything else with a price tag
- *Personal costs:* peace of mind, credit-worthiness

Reduce costs using one of these techniques:

- Reduce what you owe—Be a resident assistant, maximize credits taken per term, or get a school scholarship.
- Eliminate non-essentials—Do you really need cable or a spring break cruise?
- Choose a cheaper option—Attend a community college for two years.
- Increase your resources—Get a part-time job or find an entry-level job with tuition benefits.

How little can you spend
and still get what you need?

Managing Costs—Part II: Personal Stuff

How savvy are you about money? Are you a natural saver or a spender? Have you managed a personal budget? Do you have a good financial role model?

Whatever your answers are, start budgeting now. Saving money on college begins with an awareness of your options and how they fit your goals. A good decision for Tim may be a rotten choice for Lea.

So how do you become financially "aware"? Awareness begins with curiosity. Curious students ask questions. High-debt students tend to take any loan that is offered without asking themselves or an outside advisor if the debt makes financial sense.

Awareness also requires that you pay attention. Tuition may be the single most expensive price tag for college, but it is not necessarily where you'll spend the most money. Ask a high-debt student where the money went and, if they can remember, you'll hear about a ton of expenses that have little to do with tuition. You might be surprised how many full-scholarship students take $25k or more in loans before they realize what they've done.

Self-awareness, particularly of expectations, comes next. What are your expectations for the college experience? Do you expect college accommodations to rival a decent hotel or are you prepared to rough it for a period of time? Do you expect to travel, or be entertained, in the manner to which you've grown accustomed (i.e., on your parents' budget) or are you ready to live like a student?

If the concept of financial awareness is new, take the next month to practice. Track your expenses for a month. Notice when you choose a higher-priced option. Do you distinguish between needs and wants? What is behind your decisions? Notice the questions that cross your mind about college costs. Did you seek answers or brush them off?

The more you realize where, what and why you spend the way you do, the easier it will be to control college costs—even the big ones.

Do your expectations match your budget?

Managing Costs—Part III: College Brand and the Sales Side of School

Both sides are selling. Both sides are buying. Be proud of your acceptance letter. But know that it is more than a nod of approval. It also means they want what you bring them.

Higher education is a multi-billion dollar business in America. Brand strength impacts a school's ability to attract top students, faculty, research funding and potential employers. The achievements of students and alums add strength to their brand. You've read these stories in the marketing materials.

When you earn your degree you receive lifetime rights to use their brand name on your resume. In addition to your degree, you may also 'sell' this brand to employers or graduate programs. Thus, it is wise to bear in mind both your college major and the college brand as you decide how much debt to incur.

In the general marketplace there is simply less pay-back risk for a $75,000 loan for a finance degree from Yale than for a $75,000 loan for a fashion degree from Unranked College or perhaps Billy Ray's Online University.

For the record, brand is defined by the market. That means good brand isn't necessarily defined as, say, Harvard. Employer A may prefer graduates from public schools; or from three specific Ivy League programs; or from Billy Ray's University. If you want to target a specific employer, ask where they recruit.

To decide if brand is important for you, ask:

- Do I want my degree to attract a certain graduate school or elite employer? If so, brand may be important.
- Am I mostly interested in the college "experience"? Becoming a well-rounded person? Meeting new people? Paying the least to earn a degree? If so, brand may be less important than personal fit.

Both sides are selling. Both sides are buying. Brand matters—you decide how much.

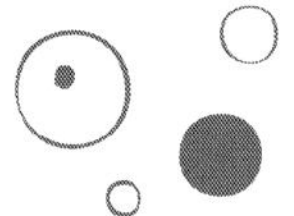

Chapter Two: The Big Things—How to Save $10,000 to $50,000

How to Save Big

Whether you are trying to reduce college costs, a family budget or the national debt, the easiest place to save big is with big hits.

Students who save the most use at least one idea from this chapter. The good news is you already know the basics.

Woohoo! Remember saving up for that LEGO Hogwarts Castle set in 3rd grade and the excitement of finding a $20 bill in a birthday card? Finding one tactic to reduce college cost by five figures is an exponentially bigger thrill.

Cost and quality. We have all splurged on something that wasn't what we expected, given the price tag. The big hits in this chapter decrease college cost without decreasing educational quality.

Personal value. A $295 backpack might be a good value to you while your best friend is ok going cheap. Separate your needs from your wants but avoid harsh tactics just to save some bucks. You aren't saving if you make cuts that don't work for you.

Give each idea in this chapter a chance, then move on. Here is a preview of tips to save big:

- Decide how much you are willing to spend and borrow for your degree BEFORE you start school.
- Create a budget. Stick to your plan.

- <u>Select federal loans first</u>. Over the life of the loans, the difference you pay back for a $20,000 subsidized[2] federal loan and a $20,000 private loan can be as much as $46,000. Saving doesn't get any easier.

- <u>Live like a student</u>. Retail ads implore you to make your dorm room look and feel "just like home" with their products. It isn't. Don't buy it (the message or the product.) Cheap creativity can be so much more fun.

- <u>Ask</u>. Actively Seek Knowledge. For instance, only those who locate and apply for scholarships have a shot at winning.

Look for the big savings opportunities first.

2. Federal *subsidized* loans are financially supported (subsidized) by the government, meaning they pay the interest on those loans for you while you are in school half-time or more. In comparison, no one pays the interest on federal *unsubsidized* loans except you. Instead the interest accrues while you are in school, increasing your balance until you begin making payments according to the contract schedule.

The New Community College

Community colleges may be the fastest growing higher education choice in the United States. Almost half of post-secondary students attend a community college. That's 12.4 million students enrolled at one of the 1,167 community colleges.

Average annual tuition and fees for in-district students to attend a public community college: **$2,713.**[3] *For the year.* ***Full-time.***

Today's community colleges are vibrant centers that offer high-quality, competitive, transferable, low-cost education to students of all ages, interests and career goals. You will find:

- *Excellent faculty*—With a reputation as approachable experts, many community college faculty chose to apply their PhDs here where they can do what they love: teach you.
- *New facilities*—Millions of dollars have been spent in recent years to upgrade classrooms, labs, performing arts centers, sports complexes, and even add dorms.
- *Academic peers*—Whether you are studying office management or plan to earn a PhD in physics you will find academic peers who challenge you.

---

3. Data on this page comes from the *2011 Community College Fast Fact Sheet,* Retrieved from www.aacc.nche.edu April 1, 2011.

- *Student associations*—Leadership opportunities are available in academic, social, professional and national honor societies, including Phi Beta Kappa.
- *Solid brand*—Given their ability to rapidly develop cutting-edge skill-based training programs, many community colleges have earned a strong reputation with local employers as lifetime learning centers.
- *Academic recognition*—Ask if the school has agreements with four-year schools that almost guarantee transfer of your credits. To sound really smart, ask about their articulation agreements.

Visit community colleges!

Community College Options

You don't have to be a full-time student to benefit personally and financially from a community college experience.

Could one of these options work for you?

- Take general credits at a community college during summers.
    - Are you a camp counselor? Ask about online classes.
- Take challenging pre-requisite courses that may require extra help.
- If you change your major half-way through, catch up with community college coursework.
- Are you curious if you'd be good at massage therapy or forensic science? Start with a class here. If you hate it, you'll be able to change directions quickly. If you love it, you'll know.

Transferability is not an absolute guarantee. Always be sure to:

- Ask the registrar at the school you want to transfer the credits to, which classes will substitute for general credits or pre-requisites in their program.
- Double-check transferability details for credit values.
- Double-check transferability for online courses.

- When in doubt, ask. Community colleges are among the most welcoming educational environments you will find.

"We are getting more [students] taking advantage of the affordable tuition and transferring to other colleges, saving $30,000 to $60,000 while achieving a four-year degree."[4]

Nicholas Neupauer, President,
Butler County Community College, Butler, PA

---

4. Grant, T., *College revenues rise on tuition, student growth*, Pittsburgh Post-Gazette, Tuesday, March 22, 2011. Used with permission.

How to Reduce Tuition Costs

Once you've chosen a college, tuition is a fixed expense, right? Not necessarily. Try one of these options[5]:

- **Get credit**—Earn up to a year of credits by taking exams before you start college. Cost is about \$75–\$90 for each exam. Scholarships may be available. Students can earn 3–12 credits per exam, as determined by each college.
    - *Advanced Placement (AP) exams*—34 exams are available based on AP high school courses. Research indicates AP students are more likely to graduate in four years and to earn scholarships. www.collegeboard.com/student/testing/ap/about.html
    - *CLEP exams*—33 exams are available in 5 subject areas. Tests are taken online and scored immediately. http://clep.collegeboard.org/
    - *DSST exams*—38 exams are available and may be fully funded for active military duty students and spouses. Test prep materials are available on their website. www.getcollegecredit.com
    - Check with your state education department for state-funded post-secondary options for high school students. Ask which programs include college and high school credit.

---

5. Always check with your target four-year school for transferability and specific rules.

- **Finish in 4 years rather than 5 or 6**—As few as 37% of traditional-age students graduate in four years.
    - Avoid the cost of an extra semester by plotting out your schedule for pre-requisites and graduation requirements.
- **Graduate one semester early**—Careful planning can net a $25,000 savings at a $50,000 per year school.
- **Maximize credit blocks**—Many colleges charge tuition in blocks rather than per credit. Tuition is the same whether you take the lowest or highest number of credits in a range. It doesn't take a math whiz to see the deal here.
- **Come prepared**—Only pay once for a course; failed courses cost double.
    - Take non-credit remedial coursework at a learning center, community college or at www.khanacademy.org (exceptional and *free* youtube-based training).

How can I maximize my tuition dollars?

Other Tuition Programs

There are more ways to get someone else to pay for your college than locating a big scholarship or a rich and generous uncle.

Review the programs in this section. Then ask if these apply to you or the college you hope to attend. Ask your school counselor, parent, teacher, financial aid officer, state representative, neighbor, a friend's parent. Start anywhere and keep asking until you have an answer.

Here are a few terms:

- *Tuition reciprocity*—an agreement between states to charge in-state tuition or offer a discount to students from the partner state
- *Tuition remission*—an agreement among colleges to offer tuition reduction to students whose parent works at a member college
- *Tuition reimbursement*—a workplace benefit for employees (Even if you have a part-time job, ask about this benefit and how to qualify.)
- *Cooperative programs*—Get paid to work in your field of study while you go to college. www.co-op.edu
- *Internship options*—It is rare but sometimes a company will offer a tuition award in lieu of salary.
- *Military*—Read about benefits at www.va.gov or contact a military education benefit expert for details.

- *Free or work-for-tuition schools*—Students at Berea College and College of the Ozarks work about 10 hours a week on campus in exchange for FREE tuition. Cooper Union is tuition-free.
- *Grandparents*—AmeriCorp now lets grandparents transfer educational benefits to grandchildren. Thanks Grandma!

None of these benefits is "free".
Someone—you, a parent, a taxpayer—
has worked long and hard to earn the right
to these dollars. If you are fortunate enough
to receive these funds, take a moment
to say thank you.

Tips for Finding Scholarships and Grants

Your guidance counselor and college financial aid representatives are the best resources for information about legitimate, worthwhile scholarships and grants. Ask about specific sources and types of funds such as:

- School-funded (sponsored by your high school or college).
- Association-funded (sponsored by a professional or academic organization such as the Rotary or the Society for Human Resource Management).
- First-year student scholarships.
- Merit-based (grades and test scores).
- Activity-based (sports, arts, etc.).
- Need-based (based on financial resources as determined by your FAFSA[6]).
- Ethnicity-related (e.g. Asian American Student Association).
- Merit/Renewable (renewed if student maintains a specified GPA).
- Department-specific (often an upperclass award).
- Special awards (may be a one-time award).

---

6. Free Application for Federal Student Aid, http://www.fafsa.ed.gov

- Competitions (e.g., writing or science contests, moot court competition).
- Obscure grants (e.g., to study golf course turf, for women helicopter pilots).

Some scholarship websites are trustworthy while others simply collect and sell your information for a profit. Before you provide personal data, read their privacy policy. Look for a TRUSTe privacy seal at the bottom of the screen. If a site feels uncomfortable (too many ads, offensive language in posts), don't give them your personal data.

A good place to look is Collegeboard's database of 2,300+ funding sources totaling more than $3 billion in aid.[7] That should keep you busy!

Try this: Get together with two friends for an afternoon. One should be very calm, practical and organized. One should be Type AAA (driven, goal-oriented, overachiever). The third should have attention deficit disorder. Your goal: Each person locates five scholarship opportunities for the other two. Print or copy the basic info and share why you think this person is a good applicant. Each of you will leave with info about ten scholarships that you might have overlooked.

Think Outside

---

the Lines

7. www.collegeboard.com; click on "For Students" and then "Pay for College."

Inside Scoop on Outside Scholarships

And now for a word about outside scholarships.[8] These are funds from organization other than your college.

- The scholarship process is a lot like job hunting. If you don't try, you can't win. But, you'll never really know how the winner was chosen over you. You may be up against one other applicant or thousands. There is no guarantee your application will even be read. Comply with all the requirements, write in the spirit of the award and then let it go. Never feel bad if you aren't selected.

- Applying for a scholarship takes time. Choose wisely. Ask yourself if the value of the scholarship, in light of the chance you'll win, is worth your time. Are you better off just earning guaranteed funds?

- Is it true that scholarship funds go unused every year because no qualified candidate applied? Yes. If you love the hunt and have time, go for it.

How are candidates selected? A lot like job candidates. Here are three models I've witnessed as a scholarship judge:

- Selection can be as simple as three judges discussing essays around a table or one person (the donor) finding the most appealing story.

8. Tuition scholarships offered on your financial aid award letter are sometimes called discounts since they represent a discounted price the school offers you.

- Company sponsors may use scholarship-specific software to have a hundred employees rate and sort thousands of applications.

- Donor organizations may opt to hire a scholarship management company to ensure non-bias in winner selection.

If you win a scholarship, celebrate! If you don't, do not despair. Not winning doesn't mean you are a loser. It means someone else's application was chosen, period. If you meticulously followed application requirements, got everything in on time and wrote in the spirit of the award, your turn will come.

My advice: find two to five scholarships that appeal to you and won't take lots of time from other important activities (such as application essays). Do your best, then let it go.

Your turn will come.

Housing—On-Campus

Unless you get a full ride including room and board, consider ways to reduce the four-year cost of housing. Start by asking about any housing policies or live-on-campus requirements

Living at home for a year can save $10,000 or more. If that works for you, fantastic. But think carefully through this decision. Even though I'd love to see you save the money, the benefits of living on campus may be better for you.

Lots of students feel living on campus is a big part of the college experience. Even community colleges in 28 states now offer students a residential option. Friends are nearby, facilities easily accessed, and there is something unique about living among fellow students.

Many people meet lifelong friends through dorm life, in spite of the plethora of bad roommate stories. Plus you can learn a ton about yourself as you share living space with people raised by different parents. Whether you are the clean one or the messy one, the early riser or late riser, it is one big learning experience.

The first year is also a time to learn what you need from your living arrangement in order to get what you want from college.

Examples of on-campus options include:

- Choose a cheaper dorm. Ask the campus housing office for options.

- Move into an on-campus specialty house.

- Live in school-managed apartments.
- Be a residence hall director.

Before you make a housing decision, ask yourself:

- Can I study anywhere or am I easily distracted?
- Do I prefer the constant buzz of a crowd or do I like quiet?
- Am I involved in on-campus activities?
- Do I spend a lot of time in the library, the student center, off campus?

Housing can profoundly affect your college career. Choose carefully.

Housing—Off-Campus

Off-campus housing can offer huge cost savings or be a money-sucking nightmare. It is also critical to understand how your living environment impacts your ability to study. Know what you need. Use caution.

The biggest off-campus cost savers are:

- *Live at home.* Recognize this still costs money, if not for you, for the head of the household; be sure to say thank you.
- *Live with a relative.* Some students save by staying with a relative who lives near their school of choice.

You could also:

- *Be a live-in nanny.* This typically covers room, board and a small salary.
- *Rent a room* in the home of a nearby senior citizen. They are typically quiet and enjoy the company.

Or you could *rent an apartment or house*. Before you run down this path, ask yourself:

- Are my potential roommates people I know *very* well and trust?
- Can we have constructive arguments?
- Whose name is on the lease?
- How will we split expenses for shared stuff such as heat, electricity, damage or toilet paper?

- Do we have similar study habits and personal goals?
- Do we have similar social habits with parties, sleepovers, smoking?
- Do we have similar ideas about how an apartment will be better than a dorm?
- What are my options if the living arrangement fails?
- When can I exercise those options? Am I stuck in a long lease or can I move?
- Would my grades be at risk if this option failed?
- What are the extra expenses I wouldn't incur in a dorm? (e.g., transportation, basic furniture, kitchen tools, heat bill)
- What are the extra tasks that require time and energy? (e.g., cooking, cleaning, shopping, house meetings)

Who can you really live with when there is no Resident Assistant to intervene?

Food

Food is good. Whatever you do, don't skimp on food. Have fun. Party on (as your grandparents used to say.)

But you ask, "How can I possibly save $10,000 on the cost of food during college?"

All it takes is to NOT SPEND $10 a day and you'll save $3,650 a year or $14,610 over four years. Save that money for a car, house, or a chunk of graduate school.

The three simple food rules for the college student are:

Rule One: *Only pay for food once.*

- If you live at home, bring a lunch and snacks. Don't buy food at the school cafeteria that you can bring for a fraction of the price.
- If you live in the dorm, know your meal plan. Use it.

Rule Two: *Avoid the campus store.*

- Unless they have coffee for a quarter.

Rule Three: *Do the math. Then live the math.*

- It all adds up. Keep track of how much you spend on edibles outside of meals for a week. Candy and soda machines, snack bars, coffee shops, fast food, pizza parlors. Even if you cut that in half you'll still save a lot over four years (plus you may avoid the dreaded "Freshman Fifteen.")

- If you don't have a meal plan, look for student events with free lunches.
- Don't forget to include drinkables in the budget. Tap water is cheaper than kool-aid which is cheaper than juice which is cheaper than Coke which is cheaper than beer which is cheaper than wine which may or may not be cheaper than hard liquor. I'm just saying . . . know where your money is going.
- Understand the difference between a splurge and a habit. Save for splurges.

Eat well. Have fun. Be healthy.

Chapter Three: The Little Things— How to Save $10–$10,000

It's The Little Things

Small expenses sneak up on you. Yet it all adds up. $10 a day equals $14,610 in four years. Imagine saving half that! Low-debt students manage small expenses as well as large ones. The first tuition bill or student loan can make it all seem like Monopoly money.

Don't be fooled! Students with Monopoly-brain blow through student loan funds and rack up credit card debt at amazing rates.

And here it is. The best piece of advice in the book. Imagine a trumpet and fireworks as you read this:

LIVE LIKE A STUDENT

WHILE YOU ARE A STUDENT

AND YOU WON'T HAVE TO LATER

Too many students try to live "in the manner to which they have grown accustomed"—a standard that probably took their parents years to reach. This concept is all well and good as an alimony standard in divorce law, but high debt-load students often forget they are, well, STUDENTS.

Retailers who help you "pimp your dorm" would love to see you share that student loan money. If only they helped you pay it back. . . .

So, go retro. Really retro. Not fancy-store, expensive retro. Take the attitude students had in the past. Be proud of how little you can spend without jeopardizing your education.

Here's how the little costs can sneak up:

> Adrian and Sianni have the same meal plan. Each student is hungry. The over-priced campus store is open. Adrian returns with a $1.95 energy bar and $18.05 in non-essentials. She uses student loan money so why think twice, right?
>
> Sianni fills her water bottle, walks to the campus store and spends $1.95 cash from her part-time job on an energy bar. She makes a mental note to save cookies from the cafeteria tomorrow.

Sianni spent $2 while Adrian spent $20. Their energy bars cost the same but the cost of their excursions ranged from $2.00–$20.00. Why? Different people make different choices for roughly the same outcome. If you don't believe me recall decisions made by friends for prom.

Live like a student.

How to Save Money on a Bunch of Little Things

Take pride in your quest to live like a student. Once you are making the big bucks go ahead and buy that daily mocha and scone. For now, eat those in the cafeteria.

If you don't believe these costs matter, spend freely for a month and watch the money disappear. Or watch students who spend freely apply for more and more student loans because they just don't know where the money went. Trust me. Four years from now you'll thank me.

- *Books*
  - Buy used books from other students, the campus store or on the Internet.
  - Share optional texts or use a library copy.
- *Fees, fees and more fees*
  - Know what each fee is on any bill from your school. If you don't understand, ask. If it is for something you don't want, ask if it is optional. Knowing this tip saved me about $100/term.
  - Understand all fees associated with every student loan you are considering. A no-fee loan might be a better deal.
- *Health insurance*
  - This may show up as a fee on your initial bill.

    - Compare school insurance to coverage on a parent's policy.
    - Make sure you aren't paying for double coverage.
- *Supplies*
    - Before buying everything suggested for a course, ask past students what they used.
    - Spend money for stuff that you'll use professionally or in multiple classes, such as a stethoscope for nursing majors.
    - Stock up on highlighters and other basics during July sales at big box retailers.
    - Ask your school about student discounts on computers, software or course-specific equipment.
- *Snacks*
    - Don't pay for food twice by purchasing snacks as a substitute for a skipped meal paid for under your meal plan.
    - Keep a stash of your favorite healthy food in your room; it can comfort body and soul.
    - Share dorm room snacks with friends but don't feed the whole dorm. Students tend to find the free food. Be friendly but frugal.
    - Buy bulk snack food on sale.

    - Stock up with after-holiday candy sales.
    - Suggest care-packages as gifts from grandparents, parents and older siblings.

- *Dorm room*
    - Just say no to the multimillion dollar retail push to make your dorm "just like home." It isn't; it can be much more fun.
    - Bring bedding and basics from home. Bring only what you need to create a quality sleeping and study environment.
    - Look on student bulletin boards for stuff seniors are selling.
    - Discover Dollar General stores. They have great deals plus they give millions to education.
    - Explore thrift shops, second-hand stores or craigslist.org.
    - Don't over-buy. Add stuff as you need it.
    - Be creative. Ask anyone who went to college before 2000 about their dorm furniture.
- *Student organization dues and events*
    - Student associations generally charge fees. Take your time deciding which group is worth your money.
    - You aren't a bad friend if you don't support every fundraiser or attend every event.

    - Choose clubs and events that help you reach your goals.

- *Transportation*

    - Own a bike, not a car.
    - If you do own a car, use it sparingly. Ask for gas money when you drive friends.

- *Clothes*

    - Shop at consignment stores like Plato's Closet.
    - Shop at discount stores such as Marshalls or TJ Maxx.
    - Go practical and comfortable; you are there to study, not run for prom queen/king.

- *Internship or job search expenses*

    - When the time comes, ask your Career Services office if they have a resume-writing workshop or reduced-cost resume service.
    - Get free business cards online.
    - Look for campus fashion events with discounts on professional clothing.

"A penny saved is a penny earned."
—Benjamin Franklin

Cheap Fun

Some of the best memories in life involve fun times in college. Fun can be expensive ($250 for a rock concert) or free. Ask anyone (including your grandparents) about a fun time in college and watch their face light up. Then ask, "What made this so much fun?" I can practically guarantee you'll hear about the people, the unexpected events or the crazy stuff they did, not how much they spent.

Real students recommend:

- Hold a theme party ('90s; '70s, Pirates of the Caribbean . . . the crazier the better).
- Make an evening of attending on-campus events.
    - Do something extra. Write a review, dress up, go out for pizza afterwards, sit with new people.
- Define "party" for yourself. Besides being illegal for underage students, alcohol is expensive. Pizza and beer are great but so are pizza and generic cola.
- That said, once you're of age, share a pizza & cheap beer.
- Host a "favorite games" night.
- Organize a movie marathon.
- Explore local bookstores, coffee shops and public libraries for free events.

- Choose a weekly all-dorm TV show to watch in the lounge with popcorn.
- Ask for a student discount everywhere:
    - Travel (air, bus, train)
    - Bowling alley, restaurants
    - Local museums, theatres, sports events
- Find a favorite spot on or off campus and take some quality time by yourself.
- Every culture, family and individual has a perspective on fun. Ask others what they do for fun, and enjoy!

May I have the student discount please?

Take Care and Save

Taking care of something is the best way to make it last longer, whether it is an iPod, friend, or your own sanity.

Take care of your stuff.

- Cared-for books sell for more.
- Lock up your bike.
- A mini-fridge can last 4 years then be sold!
- Protect your laptop.

Take care of yourself. College is stressful. Exhaustion, worry and life's challenges can take a toll on your ability to learn and to make healthy choices, personally and financially. Take care:

- Physically
    - Eat good food & drink lots of water.
    - Walk to class and use the gym.
    - Sleep.
- Academically
    - Compete only with yourself.
    - Study hard then let go.
- Financially
    - Balance cost-saving tactics with sanity-saving spending. You're in college. Buy the t-shirt & enjoy the ride.

    - Count to ten before using a credit card or spending student loan funds.

- Emotionally

    - Laugh every day; cry and shout when you need to.

    - Make time for friends, family and dates.

    - Get help if life becomes overwhelming or dark.

Love your stuff. Love yourself.

Conserve Conservatively

Live simply.

- Limit purchases. You'll be surprised how much you can live without.
- Learn to spot deals.
- Only shop when you truly need something. A deal is not a deal if it doesn't improve your life.
- Recycle. Buy stuff you need from graduating students.

Know what you need to succeed.

- Noise cancelling headphones
- Single room for sleep
- Vitamins
- Breaks
- Exercise
- Friend time
- Mindless fun time

Take advantage of unique college opportunities.

- Study abroad. Explore programs sponsored by other schools as well as yours (confirm credits will transfer.)
- Unpaid internship. A good internship can provide valuable job experience and connections.

- Spring break—Have fun, but remember the best vacations are those that don't follow you home as credit card or student loan debt.
    - Use student discounts on travel and lodging. Think youth hostel.
    - Consider a service trip.

Press pause if you need to.

- Taking time out is not the same as quitting. A family crisis, work opportunity or mental health break may be a good reason to press pause.

Do what you need to do to stay healthy.

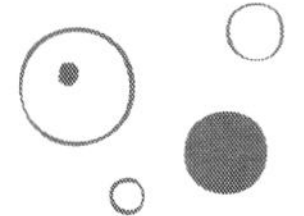

Chapter Four: Student Loans— How to Choose Wisely

Student Loan Basics

Student loans provide essential funds for many students. True, college debt is an investment in you; some say it is the best debt you can have. But it is still debt. Loans can affect your adult life or worse, outlive the life of your degree. This section teaches you the basics about controlling your debt.

The National Center for Education Statistics found that college graduates in 2008 borrowed 50% more than graduates in 1996 borrowed. There are a number of reasons for this including rising tuition costs, more low-income students in college, and student lifestyle expectations. Whatever the cause, the result is a national student loan debt of nearly $1,000,000,000,000 (one trillion dollars).

That's more than our national credit-card debt.

Quick access to private loans can give the false impression this is easy money. Student loan funds feel like a windfall whether you grew up rich or poor. Unless you are diligent, these funds will slip away on non-essentials, requiring even more loans to pay school bills.

Do you know the maximum student debt load that is reasonable for you? High-debt students rarely do. Instead, they take more and more loans to "meet their need." Determine your budget up front and stick with your plan. Chapter 7 teaches you how.

Loans are also one of the easiest places to save a ton of money. Here are a few basics about the world of student loans:

- Student loans are not charity; they are big business. You *pay* to borrow someone else's money.

- Student loans involve a legal transaction. When you sign for a loan you are signing a binding contract.
- When schools promise to "meet 100% of your need," this is not a promise of extra scholarship funding; it is a promise to help you find loans to fill a shortfall.
- Student loans are for tuition, room, board, books and related expenses. Period.
- Student loans are for you, and only you.
- Choose loans and lenders with care. Compare rates, fees, payment options. This tip alone can save thousands of dollars over the life of a loan.
- School statistics about "average student loan debt" rarely include parent loans, personal loans or some private loans.
- Student loan debt never goes away until you repay it. Even if you file bankruptcy, student loans remain. If you fall on bad times and move your family into a homeless shelter, the student loan collection company will find you. If you die, they will contact your estate. The same goes for parent loans or co-signers on your loans.
- Beware of over-zealous financial aid reps who push loans. Remember:
    - They work for the school, not you. Their job is to help you find funds (mostly in loans) that pay your cost to attend their school.
    - They don't have to pay back your loans.

Why Student Loans are a Good Idea

An international student I taught said it best, "You have such a great country that says, 'Here, take this money to educate yourself. Make something of yourself and pay it back so the next one can go.'"

Student loans allow the average individual to pursue higher education, which in turn builds a strong society. Without student loans, few could afford the training to become teachers, nurses, social workers, engineers, craftsmen, artists, scientists, attorneys, architects or doctors.

Student loans provide:

1. *Equal opportunity.* Student loans provide the financial means to access higher education regardless of one's socioeconomic background.

2. *Focused learning.* Not everyone can—or should—work full-time while attending college. Student loans make it possible to focus one's energy and effort on learning.

3. *Unique experiences.* Some opportunities such as study abroad, unpaid internships, national collegiate competitions, conferences or leadership opportunities are only available to registered college students. Your long-term career goals and personal circumstances will determine if these are worth additional student loan debt.

4. *Loan forgiveness or cancellation.* In a few rare cases, generally related to hard-to-fill public service careers, certain types of loans may be forgiven

or cancelled. Ask your financial aid office—and do your own Google research—to determine degree eligibility and career requirements.

Student loans provide a bridge to education for the average family.

Why Be Cautious About Student Loan Debt

When you turn 18 you are legally old enough to sign a student loan contract. The assumption is you are also smart enough to read the fine print—and assertive enough to ask questions

- *Student loans are a major purchase.* The price includes interest and fees. Calculate total costs to avoid sticker shock after graduation.
    - For example, one bank calculator estimates that a $50,000 loan with an interest rate of 6.8% and 20–year repayment schedule will cost $381.67 per month. The total amount you repay is $91,600.74. That's $41,600.74 you pay the lender on top of the $50,000 you borrowed.
- *Interest rates can be fixed (never change) or variable (can go up).* Know this and you'll avoid a surprise.
- *Know if you are signing for a federal loan or private loan;* federal loans generally have lower interest rates and more flexible payback options if something goes wrong. If you qualify for federal loans, always take those loans before considering a private loan.
- *Know about up-front fees.* If you borrow $5,000 from a lender with up-front fees, expect to receive less than $5,000.

- *Know if interest is waived, accrues or requires payments during school.* If interest accrues, you may be charged interest on interest until you graduate.

- *Understand when payments kick in.* Upon graduation? Six months after graduation? If you drop to less than half-time?

- *Know who you are borrowing from.* Choose a lender you trust; someone who isn't just friendly but who actually answers your questions. If you hear, "You don't need to worry about the payments until later when you make the big bucks," run, don't walk, to another lender.

Student loans may be your first binding, legal commitment. Understand your part of this contract.

Comparing Rates and Terms

The chart on the next page demonstrates how you can save money over the life of a loan by simply choosing your loan with care.

The rates in this chart are used as examples. Use reliable websites to find current rates or to do your own calculations. A few resources are in the back of this book.

If Brent takes out a private student loan for $20,000 at 12.75% interest, for a 10–year term he'll pay **$15,482 in interest** on top of the original $20,000. If Brent chooses a 25–year repayment plan, he will pay **$66,543** over the life of the loan. He'll have paid $20,000 toward the principal and **$46,543 more in interest.**

If Sam takes out $20,000 in federal subsidized loans at 6.8% interest, for a 10–year term he will pay $27,898 over the life of the loan. He pays the same $20,000 as Brent toward the principal but Sam only pays **$7,898 in interest.**

Both men get the same $20,000 in loan money but Brent's $20,000 costs him between ***$7,584 and $38,645 more*** than Sam's $20,000.

Student Loan Comparison Chart

$20,000 loan with a 10-year term[9]

	Est. Interest Rate	Monthly payment	Total Cost to You	Mark-up over the life of the loan
Federal Subsidized[10]	6.8% (in 2012)	$232	$27,898	40%
Private Student Loan	Current fixed rates are up to 12.75%	$296	$35,482 (10 yr term); $66,543 (25 yr term)	77% (10 yr term); 233% (25 yr term)

Figures were determined using a student loan calculator at www.wellsfargo.com.

The monthly payments can be deceptive. Notice how the extra $64 per month becomes thousands of dollars over time. Use a loan calculator to compare rates and total loan costs for these and other loans such as parent PLUS loans, Perkins loans and Federal unsubsidized loans.

Which loan will you choose?

9. Loan terms start counting with your first payment, typically after you leave school.
10. The government pays your interest on subsidized federal loans while you are in school. Interest on unsubsidized loans accrues the whole time.

What is Reasonable Student Loan Debt?

My rule of thumb is to use the low estimate for your first year's salary. Another is to limit yourself to federal subsidized student loans. Either rule is good. Read on for other guidelines.

What do you believe you'll be able to afford in loan payments? What feels to you like your financial and emotional limit in total student loan debt? How do you define "reasonable"? 10% of your salary? 40%? 2%?

Remember: this is just the first round. A college degree used to provide a lifelong career. Today it can launch a first career but more importantly, provide a foundation. Even without graduate school you may need funds for retraining. Keep that in mind as you decide how much loan money to take for the first round.

Below are three steps to identify a reasonable student loan debt for you. (example in italics.)

Step One: Identify the low-end expectation for a first-year salary in your field of study, adjusted for (a) the region or city where you plan to work and (b) the type of employer you will target (big business, small business, government, non-profit, your own start-up). *Let's say $35,000.*

Step Two: Multiply this number by the likelihood of getting a job in the first 3 months after graduation. Use the following criteria:

- If you have a signed offer letter multiply by 1.00 to indicate you are 100% certain of a job upon graduation. *$35,000*

- If you think you'll have a 50/50 chance, of being in the employed half of your class multiply by .50. *$17,500*

- If you plan to graduate with a high GPA, in a field with job growth, use .75 or .90. This means 3 out of 4 (or 9 out of 10) of your peers and you will get jobs upon graduation. *Using .75, your reasonable loan debt is $26,250—which is about the max for federal subsidized loans.*

Step Three: How old will you be 10–15 years after graduation? Imagine yourself with a house, car, kids. Now imagine making student loan payments for all those years.

- If you didn't blink, use the number from Step Two; $26,250 in our example.

- If Step Three made you gasp, find a number that allows you to breathe.

Just because you can [take a loan] doesn't mean you should. What is reasonable debt for you?

Student Loan Interest as a Tax Deduction

This section was written with great trepidation as I am neither a banker nor a tax expert. However, I am an expert on helping students avoid expensive errors. One of those mistakes is thinking you don't have to worry about student loan interest because it comes off your taxes. Wrong.

You may, or may not qualify for tax-related programs. Know what might be available, but never use a potential tax break to justify non-essential student loans. Even if you qualify for every tax break in existence, *you still have to make your payments.*

To give you a taste of how tax relief might work, consider how interest on qualified student loans may be deductible on your taxes. Did you catch the three fine-print terms in that sentence? If so, apply directly to law school. For the rest of you, here they are:

- *Qualified*—Most, but not all, student loans qualify for tax-related relief. Ask. Also, your loan may qualify, but you may not. Each year is different.
- *May*—Qualified student loan interest merely reduces the amount of income on which you pay taxes . . . assuming you (a) qualify by income level or filing status, (b) have income and (c) made enough taxable income but not too much.
- *Deductible*—Ask a tax professional how or whether this benefit might apply to you. According to a CPA friend:

- Definitions and tax formulas can change each year.
- Your actual benefit is determined by your tax bracket and limited by your income or tax filing status (e.g., currently married individuals filing jointly don't qualify.

Speak with a tax professional or go to the IRS website at www.irs.gov to locate information on educational expense related tax programs, including programs for which you qualify during college.

Default—the Dark Side of Student Loan Debt

Default happens when you fail to repay your loan. You do not want to be in default. There are many ways to avoid default, even in bad times.

But first you should know a few definitions:

Default—Means you haven't made your loan payment.

Deferment—An agreement you make with the lender to postpone payments for a specified period of time due to a qualifying event such as economic hardship or active military duty. Go to www.studentaid.ed.gov for details.

Forbearance—An agreement between you and the lender to suspend or reduce payments for a period of time. Forbearance may be available if you don't qualify for a deferment but may result in higher long-term costs.

IBR—Income-based repayment plans may be available on student (not parent) ***federal*** loans, not private loans. For the right people these are awesome. You pay a percent of your income. In some circumstances, debt that remains after a certain number of years *may* be forgiven. Ask for details.

Why Should I Care About Default Now?

First, because the best time to manage loan debt is before you create it. Second, because financial health is measured two ways:

1. Money you have—cash, savings, investments, retirement accounts

2. Money you can get—credit-worthiness

Default is like a sucker punch to the latter. Bad credit is easier to avoid than fix. If you default on a federal loan the government may be able to:

- Seize your tax refunds
- Garnish your wages
- Deny future federal grants or loans (including parent loans)
- Revoke a professional license
- Garnish social security payments
- Charge you the collection fees

Private lenders take action as well. Default may also affect your ability to get a mortgage, a car loan, or a job that requires a background check.

Never avoid your lender.

How to Avoid Default

- *Don't take more loans than your career path or other factors warrant.* Base your loan debt on fact, not on rumors about the big salary someone got last year. You have no idea if (a) it is true, or (b) his uncle is the CEO.

- *Don't take out more than you can visualize paying off.* If you hear yourself saying "I have no idea how I'm going to pay back these loans!", figure out another way to finish school.

- *Don't take more than your school brand warrants.* This is touchy but true. Companies expect to pay more for an Ivy League grad than someone from a fourth-tier school (or a fully online school.)

- If bad things happen during repayment (medical crisis, job loss, house burns down, bad, bad things), *call the lender early.* They may or may not be able to offer options. Either way, avoiding the lender never works. Protect your credit and your sanity . . . but you have to ask, and ask early.

- *Choose lenders and loans wisely.* Look for plans with options for deferment, forbearance or IBR (income-based repayment for federal loans).

- *Before choosing a school, ask for their default rate.* If it is above 5% ask why their students aren't repaying their loans. Top schools tend to have low default rates because their students get jobs.

- *Reduce your loan payments* by
    - Consolidating eligible loans
    - Asking your lender about reducing your payment for a period of time
    - Earning reduced interest rate for making on-time payments over a given number of months (Ask your lender.)
    - Exploring income-based repayment plans.

Be careful. Be planful.
Live your budget.

Chapter Five: How to Save Money on Graduate School During College

Paving the Way to Graduate School

Are you already thinking about graduate school? This chapter helps you save money up front, position yourself for scholarship funds, or at the very least increase your chance for admission to the school of your choice. These are ideas, not requirements or guarantees. Use the tips that are easy and helpful. Toss the rest.

Things You Know

Grades matter—Manage your time and your sanity. Care, but don't overstress about grades. If you have concerns, look for options.

- Visit the guidance, student success or tutoring office *before* your grades drop. These people are experts in learning styles and learning differences. They can help. And they think you are smart for coming in.
- Nervous about a critical course? Do you hope to go to medical school at Johns Hopkins University but are worried about your organic chemistry course? Audit the course at a community college first. You'll increase the chance of acing it later.

Test scores matter—Take advantage of free or low-cost graduate entrance exam test-prep classes at your college. Everyone who takes these tests is smart. Scoring high is more about preparation than IQ.

Things You Might Not Know

Crossover programs—If you already intend to head straight to graduate school, check out colleges that offer early entrance or crossover credit for graduate school.

- Programs may be called 3–3, 3–2, or 3–4 programs. The first number represents years as an undergraduate, the second, years as a graduate student. You save a full year of tuition and expenses.
    - Take, for example, a 3–3 program in law. Undergrads who declare an interest in law school early and are accepted into the law school, literally spend their last undergraduate year as a first year law student. One year of expenses—saved. Similar programs exist in many other fields.

Student Memberships—As an undergraduate student you'll be recruited to join many organizations. These fall into two categories in terms of their value for graduate school.

- *School-sponsored organizations*—Whether organized by community service interest, political affiliation, ethnic background, field of study or academic honors, school-sponsored organizations can offer leadership experience that bolster your graduate school application. Networking with alumni members may also lead to internships or mentors who can guide your career and graduate school decisions.

- *Professional organizations*—Join the national professional association for your field. Student cost is typically a fraction of what it will be after graduation. Plus, some groups offer graduate school scholarships for undergraduate student members. All offer great opportunities to network with people in the field, learn about hot topics, and hear about jobs.

College Choice—Now we're back to the really touchy subject. Does your choice of undergraduate college play a role in whether and where you get in to graduate school? Perhaps even influence grant money offered? Yes.

If this is important to you, ask the college admissions rep what graduate schools students frequently attend. Also know that:

- College brand affiliation is one piece of the admissions and grant-awards decision. Grades, test scores, references, entrance essay, diversity, home state, honors and achievements also matter.

- It *is* distinctly possible for a graduate from Local State College to be admitted to Harvard Law School. But statistically you can maximize your chances for Harvard Law if you attend a top-ranked undergraduate program, especially in this example, Harvard. The reasons are too numerous to describe here, but for a superb explanation complete with recent data, see the chapter titled "The Golden Dozen" in *Higher Education?*, by Andrew Hacker and Claudia Dreifus.

Study abroad—During your parents' and grandparents' lifetimes, the world transitioned from a centuries-old local economy model to a new global economy. Before the 1960s, few Americans traveled abroad except for military service. Student exchange programs expanded in the '70s and '80s but had few participants.

Today, hanging above my desk is a world map marking the countries where my four kids and I have traveled and studied: 41 countries representing every continent, and counting. Their children—and your children—will view international travel and business as routine.

What does this mean for study abroad programs and graduate admission standards?

- New expectations—Completing a study abroad no longer serves to distinguish one student from another (although the specific study abroad program may). Studying abroad is now an often-unstated expectation for elite graduate programs that seek globally-savvy, independent students.

- Some programs require fluency in one or more foreign languages, an easy requirement for international students in American colleges. Be ready to compete.

Internships—This is a two-step suggestion. You know that an internship can be an excellent way to network with professionals in your field of study (step one). You also know that networking is a good way to locate a job in your field (step two). Full-time jobs may come with graduate school tuition benefits. Do not ask about benefits during the first interview or you'll seem a bit too self-centered. The possibility is, however, another reason to find a great internship during college.

Competitions—Students who compete in a major competition in their field demonstrate commitment, talent and willingness to take personal risk. These qualities can be attractive to graduate schools. Remember, they want what you bring. If they can brag about you, they will. "Our entering class of twenty-five includes three national forensics champions, two Olympic athletes and four Fulbright recipients." Tell me you haven't read something similar in the grad school brochures.

Academic relationships—Most graduate school applications ask for a letter of reference from your undergraduate advisor, professor or department dean. Take time to develop a professional working relationship with two or three professors or administrators during your undergraduate years. The better these individuals know you, the more help they can be with your quest for further education or jobs.

Special projects—This can be a thesis, a research paper you co-author with a professor, or some other significant project that separates you from the undergraduate pack. Graduate schools look for students who go the extra mile, are creative, innovative, and not afraid to try something big.

Honors, publications, unique jobs or volunteer activities—As you walk through your four years of undergraduate education, save a document to your laptop where you keep notes of every special, noteworthy thing you do.

When it comes time to apply to a specific graduate program, look through this document. You may be surprised how many relevant activities and events you forgot about. Pick and choose the most relevant and noteworthy. If the activities and honors on your list do not relate to the program to which you are applying, ask yourself why this program is of interest to you. We tend toward activities that match our interests and develop our strengths. If you plan to go in a different direction, you will increase your chance to succeed if you know why.

It is not too early to plan for tomorrow.

Chapter Six: If You Read Only One Chapter

The Top Five Ways to Save on College Costs (and get a great education for less)

1. **Attend a community college.** Whether you take two full years of transferable coursework or a few credits during the summer, you will get a great education and save big bucks.

2. **Stick with federal loans.** Government loans are the best bet for low rates and flexible repayment options.

3. **Choose your college budget before you choose your college.** Make decisions and expenditures that honor this budget.

4. **Live like a student.** Embrace your poverty. Enjoy the benefits (youth hostels, student discounts, great excuse to go cheap) and reap the rewards down the line (manageable student loan payments, or perhaps none at all.)

5. **Spend where it matters** to you. Save where it does not. Only you can decide.

The Top Five Mistakes of High-Debt Students

High-debt students often:

1. **Choose a college based primarily on sales pitch and marketing materials.** This is just a bad idea—for anything in life.

2. **Pay no attention to their growing student loan debt or the lenders they borrow from.** "The financial aid office said I qualified so I took it." Remember the motto: Just because you can, doesn't mean you should.

3. **Do not create and follow a college budget** at any point in their college experience. They plan to worry about the debt later.

4. **Live in the manner to which they have grown accustomed, or better.** Students with the most debt perceive student loan funds as a financial windfall and spend with little thought of later consequences.

5. **High-debt students spend freely.** They fail to effectively distinguish between needs and wants, excess and necessity, essentials and non-essentials. Waste isn't viewed as a big problem.

Three Things that Impact Your Cost

Awareness | Ability to ASK | Approach

Awareness—Do you know what you want from college? The social experience? A job? A career? Any degree or a specific degree to prepare you for graduate school? All of the above? Are you and your parents in agreement about why you are going to college and what you'll get out of the experience? Have you talked about it?

Can you identify your expensive habits and personal expectations that result in purchases? With each big decision, are you aware of the options? Are you clear about which goals are truly yours and which belong to others (friends, parents, society)? As you look at each student loan, are you aware of the interest rate, term, fees and if it qualifies for consolidation or income-based reduction payments?

Students who are aware of their goals, options, budget and consequences make healthier financial decisions. High-debt students typically respond and react. They plan to worry about the details at the end. This is not a good plan for minimizing cost.

ASK—Are you willing to ASK—Actively Seek Knowledge? Students who graduate with little or no debt ask questions. Ask when you don't understand something. Ask what your options are. Ask if there are more options. Ask for suggestions to save money or find funding. Ask a financial aid officer how students with low or no debt funded school. Ask your siblings, friends, parents, clergy, mentors, neighbors how they funded college. Most importantly, ask yourself questions. What do you need (not just want)? What are the pros and cons of your choices? Ask, Ask, Ask. Then decide. (That last part is critical.)

Approach—Are you flexible? Do you hold an "I deserve only the best right now" attitude, or are you motivated to manage your expenses and have the lowest reasonable debt? Can you make the most of any situation or do you look for "things" to make you happy?

Students who are aware of options and details, who aren't afraid to ask questions, and who have a flexible, long-term approach make decisions about college costs with intelligence and intention. They know where they stand in terms of budget and debt boundaries.

For traditional-age students, the college experience is a transition to adulthood and so much more. College offers opportunities that are difficult to find elsewhere: personally, academically and simply about life. You have access to professors, science labs, art studios, library resources and much more.

Plus it is unlikely there will be another time in your life when your primary job is to learn. So learn. Learn about topics you've never heard of, places you can't find on a map and things you never knew about the real you.

College is a tremendous life-shaping gift. This is your time, your life, but also your expense. Move boldly ahead but keep one hand on your wallet.

Chapter Seven: How to Create a Reasonable College Budget

Building a Reasonable College Budget

Healthy financial decisions are made by those who know their limits *before* they shop. This chapter helps you identify a college budget that is reasonable for you and your family.

Create your budget early; if possible, do it before you apply to schools. Sit down and create it together with your parents. Allow time for discussion. Use pencil.

Just for fun, have each person answer this question:

Including cash and loans, what is a reasonable cost to you and your family for your four-year degree? $10,000? $100,000? Somewhere in between? Depends on the college? What "feels" reasonable to each of you? Share your answers, take time for conversation and write your answer(s) here___________.

Was this hard? Just imagine the challenge if subject of money isn't discussed until you have an offer letter from your #1 college choice but with far less than a full scholarship. Now things are personal.

Parents want the best for the student and the student wants to pursue his or her dreams. Big Name college wants you! You must go; you deserve to go—no matter the cost. Your future depends on it, right? Stop. Breathe. Read on.

Are *you* worth it? Yes.

But your value as a person is not the issue.

How much you and your family are willing and able to pay for your degree *is*.

College selection is an important personal and financial decision. But no single college holds the key to your life.

You do.

Building a reasonable college budget ahead of time allows you to make decisions you can be proud of down the road. The rest of this section shows you how.

Know what you can spend before you shop.

Three Family Questions (for building a reasonable college budget)

1. How much in current savings can you and your family comfortably dedicate to your degree—total? Include education savings from others (e.g., Grandma)

Student______________

Parents______________

Others______________

Comments: Before asking a parent to fork over every last dime, consider parents' retirement, savings, health care, siblings and emergency funds for a furnace or tornado damage. If there are no savings, enter zero and move on.

2. How much are you and your parents willing to commit to in loans? For how many years (loan term)?

Student loans____________(Term)__________

Parent loans[11]____________(Term)__________

---

11. Avoid parent loans and parent co-signatures in all but the most exceptional circumstances. Parents have many bills to pay. If you are a slug and default on a loan they co-signed, they have to pay it. If you die first, they may still have to pay the loan. The same philosophy goes for home-equity loans for college. Adult child/parent relationships are tricky enough without adding a multi-year debt burden to the mix. Plus the more you contribute to your education, the more you own it emotionally.

Comments: One rule-of-thumb is an estimated *starting year's salary* (more options in Chapter 4.) If your degree requires an exception to this rule-of-thumb, make sure your degree is exceptional. Use 10–year terms. Longer terms mean more years of student loan payments and more interest.

3. How much award funding can you *count on* from source such as scholarships not affiliated with a college (e.g., from Rotary, religious affiliation, high school contest or professional associations?) How many years will you receive this scholarship? Most awards are for one year, but if you received a $4,000 scholarship payable $1,000 each year, note that below.

Scholarship 1:_____total; __per year for _____ years

Scholarship 2:_____total; __per year for _____ years

Contest: _____total; __per year for _____ years

Comments: Count on is the operative phrase. If the money isn't in the bank or contractually guaranteed, put zero.

Transfer your answers to *Your Reasonable College Budget* on the next page. Use pencil or make a copy of the blank page.

Your Reasonable College Budget

Data comes from your answers to the Three Family Questions.

Source	For Bachelor's Degree	For next year
Student Savings	$	$
Parent Savings	$	$
Others' Savings	$	$
Student Loans	$	$
Parent Loans[12]	$	$
Award funds (confirmed)	$	$
TOTAL	**$**[13]	**$**

The number in the lower, right corner box is your reasonable College Budget. It comes from current data from you and your parents.

---

12. Avoid parent loans or limit them to the Parent Contribution amount on the award letter.
13. This is the total amount currently available for your college education.

Now let's look at an example. Bailey and her family identified their resources and built this College Budget.

Example: Bailey's College Budget[14]

Source	For Bachelor's Degree	For next year
Student Savings	$ 4,000	$1,000
Parent Savings	$24,000	$6,000
Others' Savings	$ 4,000	$1,000
Student Loans	$20,000	$5,000
Parent Loans[15]	$0	$0
Award funds (confirmed)	$ 2,000	$2,000[16]
TOTAL	**$54,000**[17]	**$15,000**

Bailey's budget for next year is $15,000.

Bailey is now ready to review an award letter.

---

14. Figures are fictitious and used only as an example.
15. Avoid parent loans or limit them to the Parent Contribution amount on the award letter.
16. This number reflects a one-time award or one year's worth of a multi-year award.
17. This is Bailey's four-year budget for a college degree given her current resources.

Example: Bailey's Award Letter

April 2, 2000

Ms. Bailey Student
543 Main St.
Generaltown, IL 12345

Dear Bailey:

Congratulations on your admission to Our College (OC). We look forward to working with you and your family over the next four years.

We have reviewed your application for financial aid for the next academic year. We are pleased to make this tentative[18] offer of financial aid based on a careful analysis of the information you provided.

Item	Next Year Cost at OC[19]
Tuition and fees	$32,000
Room & board[20]	$ 8,000
Books & personal[21]	$ 2,500
Travel[22]	$ 500
Total Cost	**$43,000**

18. Notice words such as "guarantee", "preliminary" or "tentative."
19. Some schools label their costs section as "Budget." Don't confuse this with YOUR budget.
20. Freshman dorm and meal plan. You might want more—or less.
21. This is the college's estimate. Your needs may vary.
22. Same as above. Change to reflect your expected travel costs.

Resources[23] and Need	
Parent contribution	$ 8,000
Student contribution[24]	$ 2,000
Total family contribution	**$10,000**[25]
Your Need = (College Cost—Family Contribution)	
Your Need = $43,000–$10,000	
Your need for next year = $33,000	

To meet your need, Our College tentatively offers you the following financial aid package. You may be eligible for more loan money. The Financial Aid Office can help you identify your maximum loan eligibility and loan sources.

Many students at Our College work part-time to cover personal costs. On campus jobs are posted online at www.ourcollege.edu/studentjobs. Upperclass students interested in jobs within their major or minor should contact the Dean of their department for an application.
(continued on next page)

---

23. This is how much the college believes you and your parent can contribute in cash *this year* based on your FAFSA data.
24. Combined with the award on the next page, Bailey is actually expected to contribute $2,000 in cash, $3,000 of work-study earnings, plus a $5,500 student loan for a total of $10,500.
25. This is likely to change a bit each year based on your FAFSA.

Source	Fall	Spring	Total
OC Scholarship	$12,250	$12,250	$24,500
Work-Study Eligibility[26]	$ 1,500	$ 1,500	$ 3,000
Federal Loan Eligibility[27]	$ 2,750	$ 2,750	$ 5,500
Total Awards:	**$16,500**	**$16,500**	**$33,000**

Contact the Financial Aid Office to complete the documents necessary to accept this award. We hope to see you this fall!

Sincerely,

Financial Aid Office

26. This is the opportunity to locate and interview for a work-study job. You must work for these funds. You may be given the choice to have earnings applied to tuition or paid to you in cash. Ask what the school's policy is, then decide what works best for you.
27. Ask if these are subsidized or unsubsidized funds. The difference is worth four years of interest.

Is The Award Enough?

Next, Bailey must determine if the award is enough, and if not, what her options are. To do this, she compares her Budget for the year ($15,000) with the total cost Our College expects Bailey and her family to pay for the year ($18,500).

Bailey's College Budget for next year: $15,000	**Our College's Cost to Bailey for next year: $18,500**
Parents: $6,000	Parents: $8,000
Bailey: $6,000 ($1,000 cash, $5,000 federal loans)	Bailey: $10,500 ($2,000 cash, $3,000 work-study, $5,500 federal loans)
Award: $2,000	
Grandma: $1,000	

Our College's cost is $3,500 more than Bailey's Budget. Plus they want Bailey to borrow $500 more in loans than she wants to take out. A total of $18,500 for a year at Our College might be a bargain—or it might not. Bailey and her family must decide what is reasonable for them.

Questions to Ask When the Award Isn't Enough

Is it worth moving forward? Is this college worth the cost to you? Is the gap small enough that there is hope? **If yes:**

- Talk to the college. Share your budget and financial changes, such as a parent's job loss, since your FAFSA was completed. Mention competitive awards from other schools. Emphasize your interest in them and what you bring. Ask them to reconsider scholarship funds.
- Does this college have other awards for which you could apply?
- Can you get more work-study hours?
- Room and board is the only realistic place to cut the award letter budget. Could you live at home or with another relative? Work as a nanny?
- Can you locate more funding? Summer job? Older sibling?
- Would the college hold your award package for a year while you worked or would they readjust the aid package?
- Could you start at a community college and transfer to this college after a year or two? Would they automatically admit you or would you need to reapply?
- Could you graduate early by earning credits by exam (CLEP, DSST, AP exams) or by

maximizing course loads? Even one semester could save Bailey $9,250 (half of the $18,500 cost.)

- Can your parents contribute real-time earnings in addition to savings allocated in the family budget? Ask if the college offers a monthly payment option.

- Are your parents willing and able to consider parent loans? Does the value of this school to you warrant parent loans?

- Do exceptional long-term benefits from this college warrant private loans?

Parent and private loans are LAST options in my view. Colleges, however, frequently suggest more loans as a *first* option after federal loans are maxed out. Loans are simply the fastest way to bridge a financial gap, especially when the student has no boundary for cost. Avoid quick solutions that have long paybacks.

Our Family's Model

College is a team effort in our family. Creating a high-level college budget for each student, each year provided a clear starting point to evaluate aid offers. This simple system was reliable and flexible. Here is how it worked:

Every December I created a Reasonable College Budget with each child for the following Fall. Financial aid forms and taxes were then easily completed by the first week in February, giving the student the best chance possible for financial aid. Next we divided college costs into two big expense buckets: (1) Tuition, fees, room and board, and (2) Everything else. We then established our budget for each of the two buckets by adding up our funding sources:

- Tuition, fees, room and board (TFR&B)—to be managed by the parents and student
    - Savings from parents and"others" (not student)
    - Student loan commitment
    - Awards
- Everything else—to be managed by the student
    - Student savings
    - Student cash (not credit) from summer jobs, small gifts, or work-study

Example: How Bailey Could Use Our Model

Using figures from her College Budget and the Award Letter:

Step One: Bailey identifies her TFR&B budget.

- $6,000 savings from parents,
- $1,000 gift from others (not Bailey),
- $5,000 in loans, and
- $2,000 from an outside scholarship award.
- Total: **$14,000**

Step Two: Bailey identifies her Everything Else budget.

- $1,000 savings from Bailey
- $3,000 Our College work-study funds
- Total: **$4,000**

Bailey's $1,000 savings can fund expenses early in the fall. Her work-study job will fund expenses during the year. If her expenses are less, she can choose to work fewer hours.

Step Three: Bailey identifies the **actual cost** for her TFR&B at Our College by copying three figures from her Award Letter into this formula:

TFR&B—Scholarship = Actual cost

$32,000 (T&F)
\+ $8,000 (R&B)
– $24,500 (OC Scholarship)
$15,500 (The basic cost for Bailey to attend Our College next year.)

Bailey and her parents notice their TFR&B budget of $14,000 (see Step #1) is **$1,500 short.** But first . . .

Step Four: What does Our College estimate Bailey will spend for Everything Else?

$2,500 (books & personal expense)
+ $500 (travel)
$3,000

Let's say Bailey needs $500 more for travel. That brings her actual expected cost for Everything Else to **$3,500.**

Good news! Bailey's actual Everything Else budget of $4,000 (see Step #2) is more than her need of $3,500. Bailey can shift the extra $500 and reduce the $1,500 TFR&B shortage (in Step #3) to **$1,000.**

Now Bailey and her family can have a discussion about $1,000. If Our College is not her first choice, Bailey may want to wait for other offers. If Our College is her first choice, she and her family can decide if $1,000 in additional expenses is possible and reasonable.

Why This Model Works:

- Students are fully responsible for managing their most flexible expenses.
- Parents and the student have already agreed on a budget for the four big costs stressors (TFR&B) when they receive the financial aid award each year or meet with the finance office.
- Each fall the student knows tuition, fees, room and board are covered for the year.

- The student can focus on studying and managing variables she can influence: personal expenses, books, travel.

- Student loan debt is tracked and manageable, even in down times. Graduation day is a celebration free from concern about unclear debt loads.

- Students and parents quickly know the size of any shortfall. In Bailey's case she knows she is tackling a $1,000 problem. High-debt students guess at how big the shortfall really is; their plan—take more loans.

- **Students graduate with four years of experience managing finances and learning to live within a budget.**

Worksheet for Our Family's Model[28]

Fill in the blanks below using your College Budget and an Award Letter. Make copies or use pencil.

Tuition, Fees, Room & Board Analysis (TFR&B)

(From Step #1)
Figures are from your Reasonable College Budget for next year:

Parent savings $__________
Others' Savings $__________
(not student)
Student Loan $__________
Outside Awards $__________

Family Budget $__________

(From Step #3)
Figures are from your financial aid award letter:

Tuition $__________
Fees $__________
Room $__________
Board $__________

Subtotal $__________
- College Scholarship $__________

TFR&B Cost $__________

Family Budget $__________
- TFR&B Cost $__________

Balance (+/−)$__________

A negative balance indicates a shortfall for TFR&B.

28. Feel free to make copies of this blank form.

Worksheet for Our Family's Model (continued)

Everything Else Analysis

(From Step #2)
From your Reasonable College Budget for next year and the financial aid award letter:

Student savings $________
Work Study award $________

Student Resources $________

(From Step #4)
From your financial aid award letter, adjusted for your needs:

Books $__________
Personal expenses $__________
Travel $__________

Student Expenses $__________

Student Resources $__________
– Student Expenses $__________

Balance (+/–)$__________

A negative balance indicates a shortfall for Everything Else.

Worksheet for Our Family's Model (continued)

How Your Budget Compares With This Offer

TFR&B Balance (+/–)$________
– Everything Else (+/–)$________

(+/–)$________

A positive number or zero means your cost is within your budget! A negative number tells you how short you are to stay in budget. Use this number to speak with financial aid or to decide if it is possible and reasonable to find the extra money.

Example: Bailey's Worksheet Using Our Family Model

**Tuition, Fees, Room & Board Analysis*
(TFR&B)**

(From Step #1)
Figures are from your Reasonable College Budget for next year:

Parent savings	$ 6,000
Others' Savings (not student)	$ 1,000
Student Loan	$ 5,000
Outside Awards	$ 2,000
Family Budget	$14,000

(From Step #3)
Figures are from your financial aid award letter:

Tuition and Fees	$32,000
Room and Board	$ 8,000
Subtotal	$40,000
– College Scholarship	$24,500
TFR&B Cost	$15,500

Family Budget	$14,000
– TFR&B Cost	$15,500
Balance	**–$1,500**

At this point in the calculation, Bailey is $1,500 short for TFR&B. Her next step is to analyze Everything Else.

*Some categories are combined to reflect the categories used by Our College.

Bailey's Worksheet Using Our Family's Model (cont.)

Bailey's Everything Else Analysis*

(From Step #2)
From your Reasonable College Budget for next year and the financial aid award letter:

Student savings	$1,000
Work Study award	$3,000
Student Resources	$4,000

(From Step #4)
From your financial aid award letter, adjusted for your needs:

Books and Personal	$2,500
Travel	$1,000**
Student Expenses	$3,500

Student Resources	$4,000
– Student Expenses	$3,500
Balance	**$500**

Good news! Bailey has $500 extra in resources. In the next step Bailey will see exactly how her budget compares to the offer from Our College.

*Some categories are combined to reflect the categories used by Our College.

**Bailey added $500 to Our College's expected travel budget to reflect her actual need.

Bailey's Worksheet Using Our Family's Model (cont.)

How Bailey's Budget Compares With the Offer from Our College

TFR&B Balance	–$1,500
– Everything Else	$500
	–$1,000

Bailey is $1,000 short of her budget. Bailey and her parents can use this number to speak with financial aid or to decide if it is possible and reasonable to find the extra money.

Student Loan Tracking Form

Use this form to keep a running tally of how much you have committed to repay in student loans. Update each term. Feel free to share copies of this blank form with friends.

Loan Amount	Date Taken	Minimum Payment (monthly)	Interest Rate	Term (yrs.)	First Payment Due
Total=		Running total of monthly payments=			

Resources

The resources in this section are examples of websites I find helpful, interesting and professional. There are many more.

Be cautious about pop-up ads for scholarship money. If it sounds too good to be true, it probably is. NEVER pay to get a list of scholarships. These are available for free.

Likewise, only share personal information with sites that are secure and legitimate. Ask a guidance counselor or the Better Business Bureau if you are unsure.

Finance and Student Loan Websites

www.Finaid.org, Begun in 1994 as a public service, this award-winning site is well worth your time.

www.studentaid.ed.gov, Student Aid on the Web, is the official site of the U.S. Department of Education. You can link to the Free Application for Federal Student Aid (FAFSA), **www.fafsa.ed.gov**, and find up-to-date information on funding higher education.

www.StudentLoanBorrowerAssistance.org The National Consumer Law Center sponsors this site to inform students with current loans about their options and rights.

www.irs.gov/publications The IRS publication, *Tax Benefits for Education*, is free here.

For an excellent sample financial aid award letter with pop-out text-box explanations go to the Massachusetts Institute of Technology site at **www.mit.edu**. Search for "sample award letter."

Each state's Office of Higher Education provides information for students and parents. For an example, go to **www.ohe.state.mn.us** and click on "Students and Parents."

Other Useful Websites

The American Association of Community Colleges, **www.aacc.nche.edu**, is the best place to learn about U.S. community colleges.

Advanced Placement (AP) course and exam information is available at: **www.collegeboard.com/student/testing/ap/about.html**

College Level Examination Program (CLEP) information is available at: **http://clep.collegeboard.org/**

Dantes Subject Standardized Tests (DSST) information is available at: **www.getcollegecredit.com**

Information on education benefits from the U.S. military is available at: **www.va.gov**.

The National Center for Educational Statistics is the primary federal entity that collects and analyzes U.S. educational data. This site contains an excellent college selection tool titled "Find the right college for you" at **http://nces.ed.gov/collegenavigator/**

The report, *Help Wanted. Projections of Jobs and Education Requirements through 2018,* issued by Georgetown University Center on Education and the Workforce is available free at **http://cew.georgetown.edu/**

The Institute for College Access and Success, **www.ticas.org**, is a non-profit organization working to make college available and affordable. Their *Project on Student Debt* offers legislative updates, loan data and tips to manage loan debt at: **www.projectonstudentdebt.org**

The College Board Advocacy and Policy Center, **www.advocacy.collegeboard.org,** offers excellent information on many topics including college success, for-credit exams (CLEP and AP) and a database of $3 billion in scholarship funds at: **http://apps.collegeboard.com/cbsearch_ss/welcome.jsp**

The *Reach Higher America* report provides data and predictions used in many educational initiatives. The report is available at: **www.nationalcommissiononadultliteracy.org**

About the Author

Laura H. Gilbert, Ph.D., is a frequent blogger, speaker and consultant on higher education. Troubled by recent stories of egregious student loan debts, Laura was inspired to create a set of books to help. "How to Save $50,000 on College," the first in this set, is written for the traditional-age student and his or her family. Other works in the set address graduate school and the financial challenges for adult learners.

Each book offers common-sense tips that come from Laura's personal experience as a professor, coach and parent of four college-educated young adults.

As an advocate for learning across the lifespan, Laura is actively involved in policy research, writing, and consulting. She also teaches organizational leadership, human resource management and psychology at undergraduate and graduate levels. Laura lives with her family in Minnesota.

Email Laura at laura@saveonyoureducation.com or follow her on Twitter at lauragilbertphd.

Laura also posts news and tips for traditional-age students at her adult-learner web site, www.backtoschoolforgrownups.com. Click on the "Trad Students" tab or search on "traditional-age students" for articles and posts relating to 16–24 year-olds.

8097344R0

Made in the USA
Charleston, SC
08 May 2011